HEALTH HEROES

I'M A FLIGHT NURSE

LAUREN KUKLA

ILLUSTRATED BY TOM HEARD

MAYO CLINIC PRESS KIDS

With gratitude to Kimberly Runnells, RN

MAYO CLINIC PRESS KIDS | An imprint of Mayo Clinic Press
200 First St. SW
Rochester, MN 55905
MCPress.MayoClinic.org

To stay informed about Mayo Clinic Press, please subscribe to our free e-newsletter at MCPress.MayoClinic.org or follow us on social media.

For bulk sales contact Mayo Clinic at SpecialSalesMayoBooks@mayo.edu.

Proceeds from the sale of every book benefit important medical research and education at Mayo Clinic.

ISBN: 9798887701080 (paperback) | 9798887701073 (library binding) | 9798887701530 (ebook) | 9798887701240 (multiuser PDF) | 9798887701097 (multiuser ePub)

Library of Congress Control Number: 2023024680
Library of Congress Cataloging-in-Publication Data is available upon request.

TABLE OF CONTENTS

CHAPTER 1

HELLO!

Hello! My name is Jessica Abrams. I'm a flight nurse! I provide nursing care to people while they are being moved in a helicopter.

I love my job because every day is different. No matter what the situation is, I always do my best to take care of my patients!

Flight nurses often work for hospitals. Some flight nurses work with the military. Others work with search and rescue missions.

I am part of the medical flight crew for a large hospital. My team and I are trained to care for patients while they are in the helicopter.

CHAPTER 2

A FLIGHT NURSE'S TOOL KIT

Being a flight nurse takes special skills. Flight nurses need to have compassion and show teamwork. We need to be able to think quickly. But there are also tools that help me do my job.

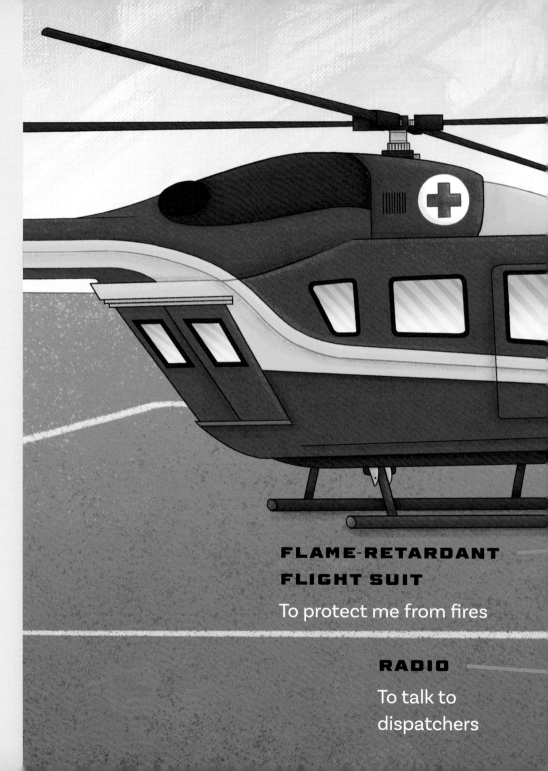

FLAME-RETARDANT FLIGHT SUIT

To protect me from fires

RADIO

To talk to dispatchers

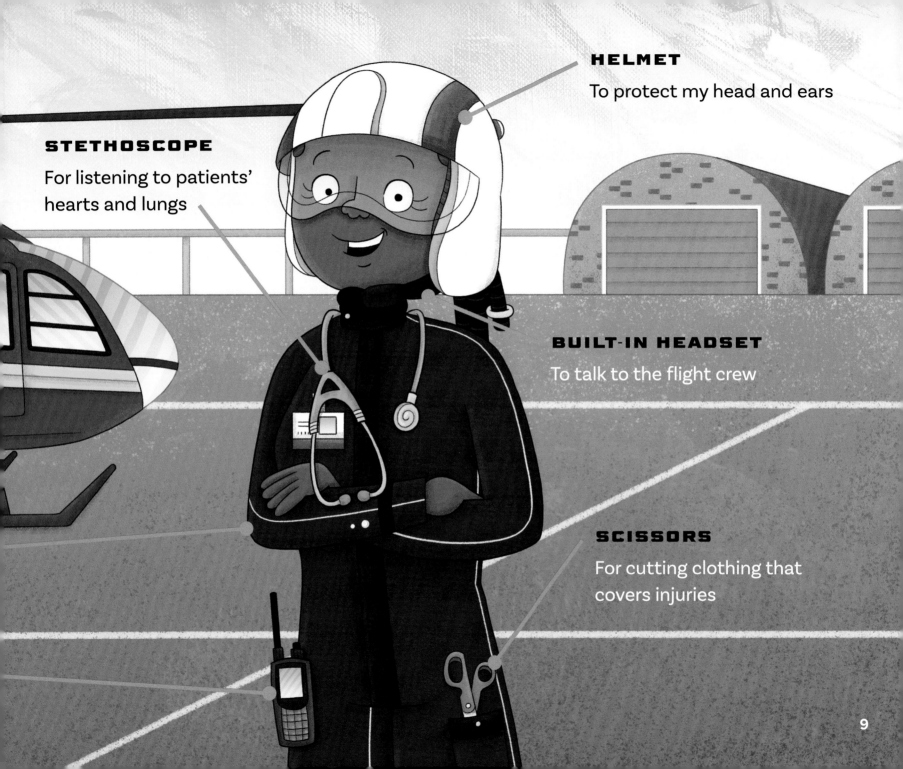

HELMET
To protect my head and ears

STETHOSCOPE
For listening to patients' hearts and lungs

BUILT-IN HEADSET
To talk to the flight crew

SCISSORS
For cutting clothing that covers injuries

I work with other healthcare, flight, and emergency workers to take care of our patients. **Meet some of the people on my team!**

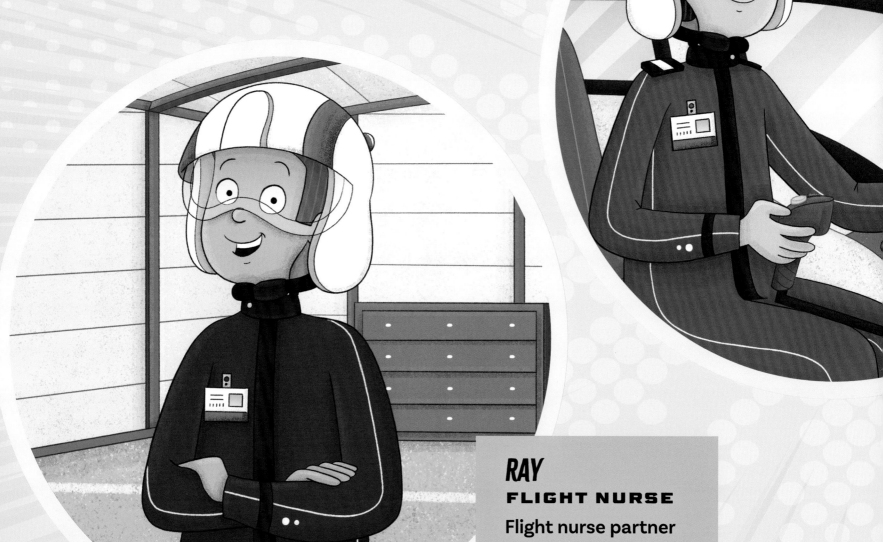

RAY
FLIGHT NURSE
Flight nurse partner

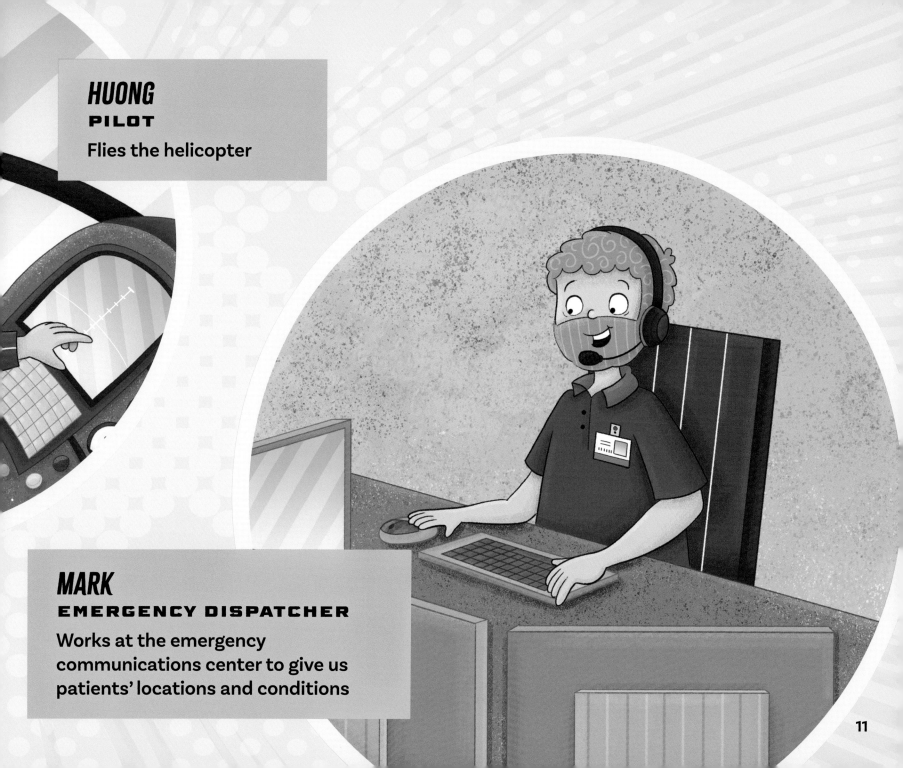

HUONG
PILOT
Flies the helicopter

MARK
EMERGENCY DISPATCHER
Works at the emergency communications center to give us patients' locations and conditions

11

CHAPTER 3

A DAY AS A FLIGHT NURSE

I usually work a twelve-hour **shift**. My shift starts bright and early in the morning.

6:50 AM

The hospital I work for has an office at a nearby airport. It also has a hangar. This is where our helicopter is kept. I park my car in the airport parking lot when I arrive.

7:00 AM

My partner, Ray, and I meet with the previous shift's flight crew. It was a quiet night. They only had one call!

13

7:10 AM

My flight crew has its morning meeting. We talk to the emergency communications center. We check in with flight teams based at other airports. Huong is our team's pilot. She lets us know it is a good day for flying!

7:30 AM

Ray and I check our supplies. We make sure no medications have expired. We check that any batteries are fully charged. Ready to go!

15

8:45 AM

Mark radios us from the emergency communications center. He says a four-year-old named Sophie is having trouble breathing. He tells us where she is. A tractor tows the helicopter out of the hangar. We lift off!

EMTs are already caring for Sophie. They tell me Sophie's breathing is better. But she needs to get to a hospital right away.

"My name is Jessica," I tell Sophie's mom. "This is my partner, Ray. We're going to fly you and Sophie to a hospital."

8:50 AM

9:05 AM

We strap Sophie to the helicopter's cot. We attach the cot to the helicopter's floor. Ray and I **sedate** Sophie. Then we insert a plastic tube into Sophie's throat. This will help her breathe.

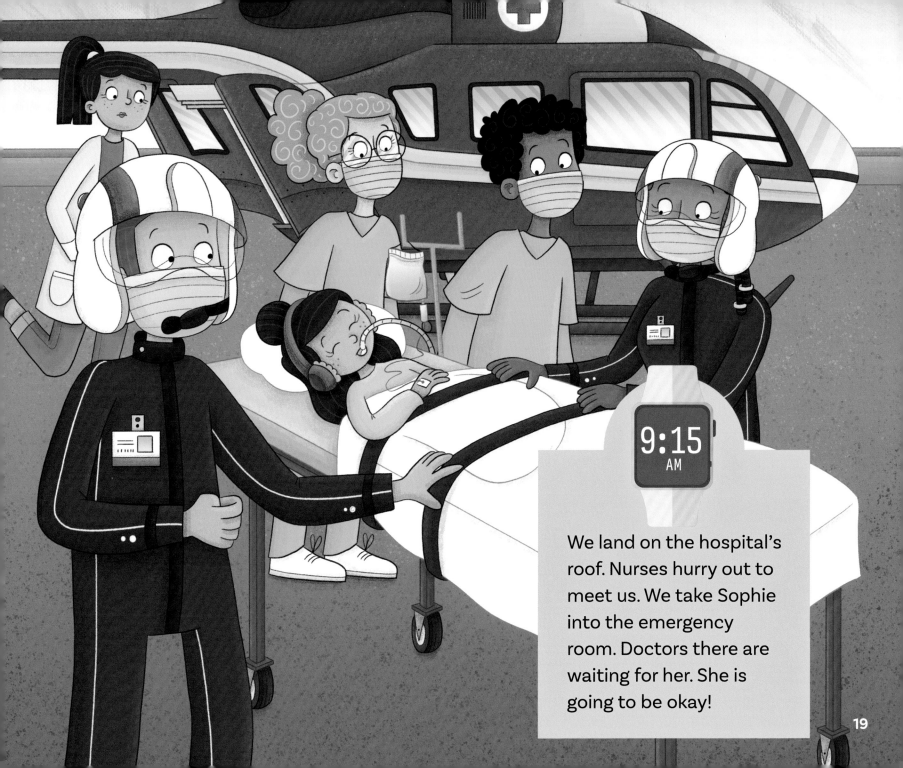

We land on the hospital's roof. Nurses hurry out to meet us. We take Sophie into the emergency room. Doctors there are waiting for her. She is going to be okay!

9:15 AM

19

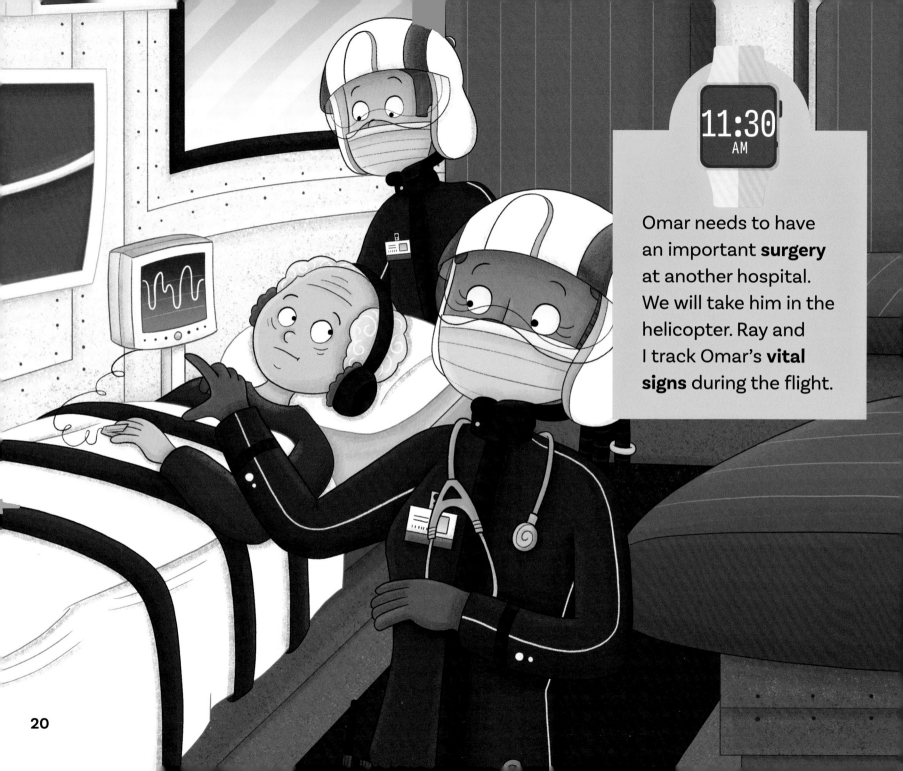

11:30 AM

Omar needs to have an important **surgery** at another hospital. We will take him in the helicopter. Ray and I track Omar's **vital signs** during the flight.

2:45 PM

Ben was stung by a bee. He had a serious **allergic reaction**. An ambulance couldn't reach his **remote** location. But the helicopter can! Ray and I give Ben medicine. We fly him to the hospital.

5:00 PM

Patricia was having chest pains. She went to her local **clinic**. The clinic's doctors called for an emergency helicopter. Patricia is having a **heart attack**. She needs to get to a hospital right away!

5:20 PM

We bring Patricia to the hospital. We tell her doctors and nurses there how she is doing. Patricia will get the care she needs.

23

CHAPTER 4

PATIENTS COME FIRST

Our shift is almost over. Ray and I restock supplies. We put away our helmets. Another call comes in!

The next flight crew isn't ready yet. So Ray and I grab our helmets. We jump in the helicopter. If patients need us, our job isn't done!

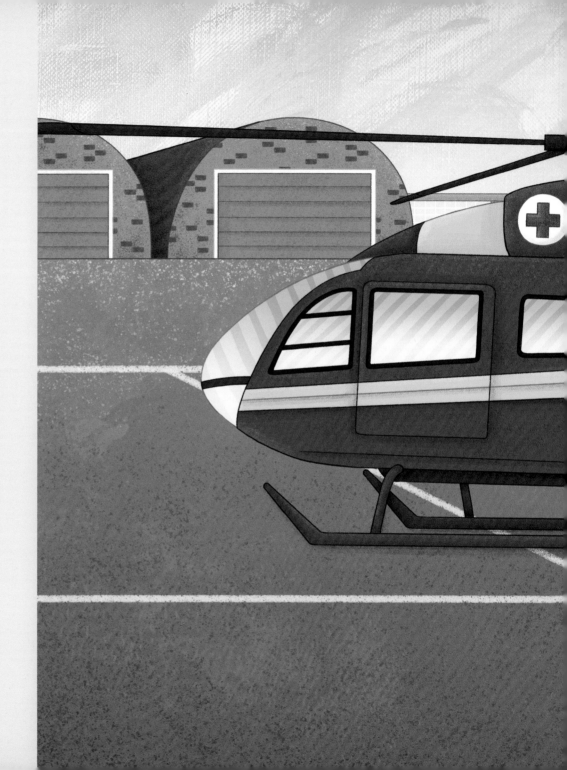

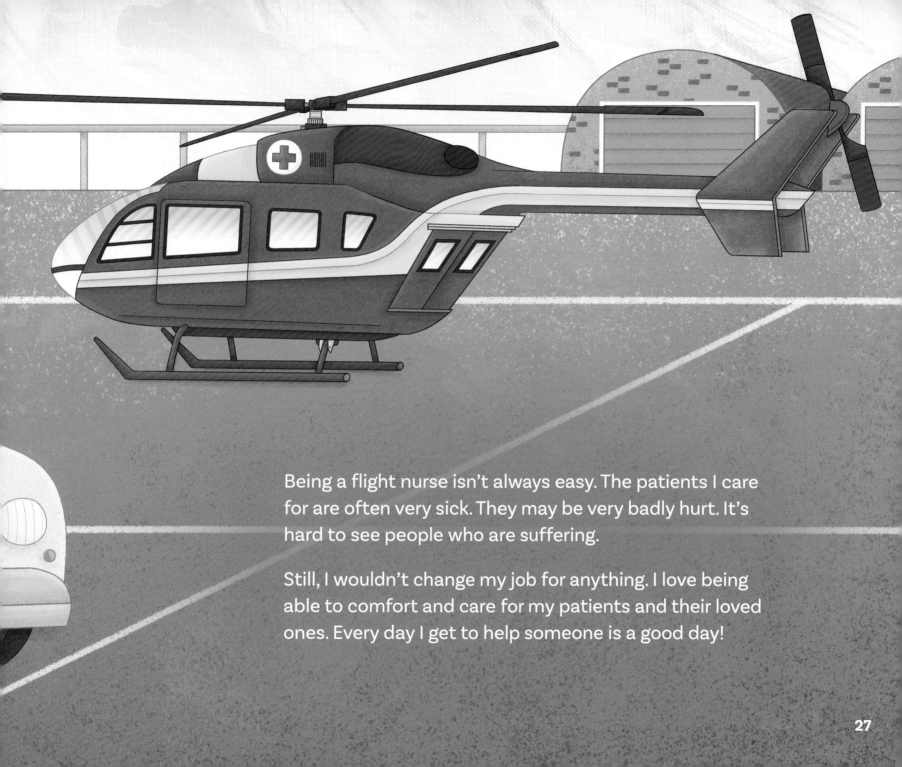

Being a flight nurse isn't always easy. The patients I care for are often very sick. They may be very badly hurt. It's hard to see people who are suffering.

Still, I wouldn't change my job for anything. I love being able to comfort and care for my patients and their loved ones. Every day I get to help someone is a good day!

REAL-LIFE HERO!

MEET A REAL-LIFE FLIGHT NURSE!

NAME: Kimberly Runnells

JOB: Critical Care Nurse

PLACE OF WORK: Mayo Clinic

What is your favorite part of being a flight nurse?

I enjoy taking care of patients and keeping them safe and comfortable. Any time I get to do that, it's a good day, no matter how challenging it was.

What does a flight nurse do?

A flight nurse is responsible for keeping patients safe and comfortable in a helicopter on the way to a hospital. We treat any immediate medical issues and monitor the patient during the flight. We deliver the patient to the hospital, where doctors and nurses there can continue caring for them. An important part of my job is keeping patients and their families calm. I ask if they have any questions and try to help ease any fears they have.

What is the hardest part about being a flight nurse?

I cannot "fix" everyone. Sometimes all I can do is provide comfort.

What character traits do you think it's important for flight nurses to have?

To do this job well, flight nurses need to be very **flexible** and open-minded. Sometimes we get a request for one thing, but when we reach the patient, the plan needs to change quickly. We need to be able to think on our feet.

SUPERPOWER SPOTLIGHT

Health heroes have special superpowers that help them do their jobs. One of a flight nurse's most important superpowers is teamwork! I work with lots of different people in my job. I listen carefully when someone is talking to me. I am helpful and kind to other people on my team. By working as part of a team, I can provide my patients the best care possible.

HOW DO YOU SHOW TEAMWORK?

TEAMWORK

GLOSSARY

allergic reaction—a response that occurs when the immune system attacks a substance that a person is allergic to. Allergic reactions can be mild or very serious.

clinic—a healthcare building where patients have scheduled visits with healthcare providers

EMT—emergency medical technician. An EMT is a healthcare professional that gives emergency care to patients and often works in an ambulance.

flexible—able to change plans or actions quickly in different situations

heart attack—a medical emergency that occurs when the flow of blood to the heart is blocked

remote—very distant from cities and towns and sometimes difficult to access

sedate—to calm someone or put them to sleep with a drug

shift—a scheduled period of time that a person is at work

surgery—a medical procedure where doctors treat or diagnose conditions, usually done after a doctor has given the patient medicine to make them sleep

vital signs—measurements of a patient's basic functions, such as heart rate, blood pressure, and temperature

LEARN MORE

Austin, Mike. *Hooray for Helpers!* New York: Random House, 2020.

KPBS Public Media. "San Diego Flight Nurse Dubbed 'Godmother of Air Medical Services' Has No Plans of Slowing Down." https://www.youtube.com/watch?v=KXTBGYtHkvs

Moening, Kate. *EMTs*. Minneapolis: Bellwether Media, 2021.

Time for Kids. "I'm a Flight Surgeon." https://www.timeforkids.com/your-hot-job/articles/my-cool-job-flight-surgeon

Wonderopolis. "Do All Heroes Have Superpowers?" https://wonderopolis.org/wonder/Do-All-Heroes-Have-Superpowers

INDEX